How to Pray the Liturgy of the Hours

Judith Kubicki, CSSF

BOOKS & MEDIA
Boston

ISBN 0-8198-3381-9

Cover design by Helen Rita Lane, FSP

Printed and published in the U.S.A. by Pauline Books & Media, 50 Saint Pauls Avenue, Boston MA 02130-3491.

www.pauline.org

Pauline Books & Media is the publishing house of the Daughters of St. Paul, an international congregation of women religious serving the Church with the communications media.

2 3 4 5 6 7 07 06 05 04 03

"I'd like to pray the Liturgy of the Hours, but...it seems so complicated. How do I begin?"

How many times have you picked up a copy of *Christian Prayer* only to put it down again, confused by Commons and Propers, Invitatories and Antiphons? Initially, *Christian Prayer* can be intimidating. Fear not, however—it's not as complicated as it may first appear.

This small booklet is designed to help you learn to pray the Liturgy of the Hours. By introducing you to its various components and explaining—step by step—how to get started, this guide offers the map for a prayer-journey that can become part of the rhythm of your daily life.

Why Pray the Liturgy of the Hours?

Every baptized person is a member of the common priesthood of Jesus Christ. Because of this, we have the privilege and responsibility to lift up the world to God in prayer. The Liturgy of the Hours provides us with the opportunity to fulfill this priestly office by using a prayer form that is one of the ancient treasures of the Church. A good deal of the prayer is taken directly from the Sacred Scriptures, both the Old and New Testaments. The readings give us the opportunity to listen to the Word of God and ponder it is our hearts. The psalms are the heart of the daily prayer of the Church. These ancient songs or prayer-poems express the entire gamut of human emotion—from the depths of lament to the heights of ecstatic praise. In praying the Hours, we use the inspired words of Scripture to address the Father in the very words Christ used when he prayed. Furthermore, we believe that the authors of the Scriptures wrote under the inspiration of the Holy Spirit. Just think about it; using this prayer, which largely consists of Scriptural texts, we actually participate in the loving communion that exists among the persons of the Blessed Trinity!

Thus, the Liturgy of the Hours deserves our highest esteem. Along with the Eucharist and the other sacraments, it is part of the official worship of the Church, that is, her liturgy. Since the Hours are liturgical prayer, the ideal way to pray them is together with other people. Nevertheless, even when we pray the Hours alone, we are united with the entire Church and all creation in offering praise and thanks to the Father, through the Son, and in the Spirit. Our individual voice becomes a part of the countless voices throughout the world that daily offer this prayer to God on behalf of the Church.

We human beings are both body and soul. This is why prayer that involves our five senses and that includes other people makes it easier for us to express our faith and to nurture it. We can do this by celebrating the Hours with symbols that engage our whole person—spirit, imagination, body, and senses. These symbols include the Word of God, light and darkness, incense, time itself, and the particular gestures of prayer such as sitting, bowing, and standing. Attentiveness to these enriches our experience of a prayer that reflects the very rhythm—the day, week, seasons, year—of our lives and the cycles of creation.

A Brief History of the Liturgy of the Hours

Scripture admonishes us to "pray always" or "pray without ceasing" (1Thes 5:17). Early Christians, particularly those who grew up in Judaism, were schooled in the Jewish practice of praying at specified moments throughout the day. These times of prayer corresponded to the Roman divisions of the day. The ancient law of the Old Testament prescribed offering the sacrifice of a lamb and the offering of incense twice a day. From the first to the fourth centuries, the early Church adopted this practice of associating prayer with these times of the day. At first, this practice was somewhat unstructured and varied from place to place. What slowly developed was private prayer in the morning and evening. The psalms and other excerpts from Sacred Scripture formed the core of these periods of prayer.

By the fourth century, two very different styles of this prayer gradually took shape, the *cathedral office* or the *ecclesiastical office* and the *monastic office*. The cathedral office was the prayer of the local church. That is, both clerics and laity gathered around their bishop for daily prayer. The monastic office, on the other hand, was the prayer of a particular community of monks. Both the ritual and the purpose of these two approaches to prayer were quite different.

The cathedral office was a highly structured prayer that included many invariable or repetitive elements. Psalms were chosen for their appropriateness to the hour of the day, the feast, or the season. For example, Psalms 63 and 51 were key morning psalms; Psalm 141, the evening psalm. The cathedral office, with its focus on celebration, employed music and colorful ceremony, including the lighting of lamps and the burning of incense, which appealed to the worshiper's imagination and five senses.

The monastic office was also highly structured. However, the principles governing its organization were quite different. The entire psalter was recited *in cursus* every week. That is, the monks began with Psalm 1, continued in sequence to Psalm 150, and then began the cycle again. In addition, the monks practiced what is referred to as *lectio continua*, the sequential reading of Scripture. One book of the Bible was read from beginning to end before another was begun. The monastic office was characterized by a minimum of ceremony. Eventually, the singing of the psalms gave way to recitation by a single monk. The focus was on meditation and edification; the psalms were a means for sustaining contemplation rather than for praise.

Eventually, some desert monks began to live in cities, and an urban monastic office replaced the cathedral office. By the medieval period, the prayer had become the reserve of clergy and religious. What had once been the public prayer of the entire Church became, for the most part, the private prayer of the clergy. Priests and religious prayed what was then referred to as the "Divine Office" in Latin. Although the laity occasionally participated, it was usually with the sense that they were joining in the prayer of a particular community, rather than in a prayer that belonged to them by reason of their baptism. Attention to the ceremony or ritual aspects of the prayer diminished or disappeared completely. Focus was placed on the book and the obligation of clergy and religious to pray it.[1] As a result, what had been ritual prayer or liturgy began to be seen as an obligatory recitation of prescribed prayer texts. While several attempts were made to reform the office, none resulted in substantial changes.

It was one of the goals of the liturgical renewal of the Second Vatican Council to retrieve the daily prayer of the Church for the whole people of God. *The Constitution on the Sacred Liturgy* (*Sacrosanctum Concilium*, 1963), specifically mentioned that "the laity, too are encouraged to recite the divine office, either with the priests, or among themselves, or even individually" (n. 100). Furthermore, the *Constitution on the Sacred Liturgy* indicated that when the office was to be revised, "its venerable centuries-old treasures are to be so adapted that those to whom it is handed on may profit from it more fully and more easily" (n. 90).

The reform of the Divine Office, now referred to as the Liturgy of the Hours and published under the title *Christian Prayer*, achieved some measure of success. The restoring of the traditional sequence of the hours—Morning Prayer prayed in the morning and Evening Prayer in the evening[2]—was an significant step toward celebrating the symbol of time with greater meaning and respect. Designating Morning and Evening Prayer as the two hinges of the day likewise restored these two hours to their rightful place of importance. Expanding the cycle from one week to four, and allowing for the use of the vernacular (the language of the people rather than Latin), have also been positive steps toward renewing this prayer for the life of the Church. However, the effort to preserve much of the tradition and to provide for a greater variety of options have made for a more challenging prayer.

This booklet provides a road map through the maze of directions and options involved in praying the Liturgy of the Hours. Primary attention will be paid to Morning and Evening Prayer, with some brief comments about Night Prayer.[4]

One note before we begin: reading the material in this booklet and observing directives can be important, but the most important aspect is the experience of prayer. Giving undue importance to guidelines and directives can get in the way of prayer. The worship of God is the ultimate goal. Learning and following the roadmap are a means to the goal not ends in themselves. So be gentle with yourself as you unpack the beauty and complexities of this ancient, but renewed prayer of the Church.

A Look at the General Contents

Most editions of *Christian Prayer* are similarly organized. Key sections (page numbers correspond to the edition published by Pauline Books & Media) can be found in the following order:

1. An abridged version of **key Church documents,** including guidelines (pp. 727).
2. A listing of **principle feasts of the liturgical year** with annual dates (pp. 28–29), and the **General Roman Calendar** (pp. 31–36).
3. The **Proper of the Seasons,** which includes prayers assigned to particular days arranged according to the chronology of the liturgical year: Advent and Christmas season (pp. 37–215), the first nine Sundays of Ordinary time (pp. 216–222), the Lenten season (pp. 223–305), Holy Week (pp. 306–347), the Easter season (pp. 348–476), the sixth through thirty-

fourth Sundays of Ordinary time (pp. 499–519), and Christ the King (pp. 520–530).

4. **Solemnities of the Lord During Ordinary Time,** which includes Trinity Sunday (pp. 467–476), Corpus Christi (pp. 477–488), and Sacred Heart of Jesus (pp. 489–498).

5. The **Ordinary** (pp. 531–546), which is a key section of the book. The order of Morning Prayer (pp. 538–541) and Evening Prayer (pp. 543–546) are outlined with commentary, and the two Gospel canticles are printed in full. Take some time to study these pages and refer to them often.

6. The **Four-week Psalter** (pp. 449–1007) comprises the central portion of *Christian Prayer*. Beginning with Evening Prayer I for Sunday (prayed on Saturday evening), it includes Morning and Evening Prayer for each day of the four-week cycle.[3]

7. **Night Prayer** (pp. 1008–1044).

8. **Complementary Psalmody** (pp. 1045–1054) for Mid-Morning, Midday, and Mid-Afternoon prayer.

9. The **Proper of the Saints** (pp. 1055–1308) includes prayers for various feast days of saints on the Roman calendar.
10. The **Commons** (pp. 1309–1432) provide prayers and readings for feast days that do not have their own prayers.
11. **Office of the Dead** (pp. 1433–1457).
12. A selection from the **Office of Readings** (pp. 1461–1733).
13. **Supplementary material** and **indices** (pp. 1734–1758).

The Basic Structure of Morning and Evening Prayer

Morning Prayer and Evening Prayer are organized according to a four-week cycle. Every four weeks the same schedule of psalmody, readings, and prayers is repeated. Solemnities, feasts, and special seasons of the year may interrupt, but the four-week pattern is the fundamental structure.[4] The structure is listed as follows:

Morning Prayer	**Evening Prayer**
Opening Verse	Opening Verse
Hymn	Hymn
Psalm one	Psalm one
Old Testament Canticle	Psalm two
Psalm two	NewTestament Canticle

Reading

Response

Gospel Canticle
(Zechariah)

Intercessions

Lord's Prayer

Closing Prayer

Dismissal

Reading

Response

Gospel Canticle
(Mary)

Intercessions

Lord's Prayer

Closing Prayer

Dismissal

In addition to these main elements, there are some other, optional elements. A brief psalm-prayer may follow the psalms, and Morning Prayer may be introduced by an invitatory psalm, which precedes the hymn (pp. 533–534).[5] Each psalm and canticle is introduced by an antiphon, prayed before the psalm or canticle, and repeated at the end if desired. No need to worry, however. All of this is clearly laid out for you in the book. Simply follow the prayer as it is printed.

Spend some time looking through your copy of *Christian Prayer* to become familiar with the basic four-week cycle of psalms, canticles, readings, and prayers. You may want to "practice" with the Morning and Evening Prayer for a given weekday before attempting the variations that come with particular liturgical feasts.

Begin to Pray!

Now that you have some familiarity with the layout of the book and the structure of Morning and Evening Prayer, let's try to pray one of the Hours. This section will walk you through Morning Prayer for the tenth Sunday in Ordinary Time as a model for praying this Hour privately. Most of the comments, however, apply to a communal celebration as well.

Some of the following information is printed within *Christian Prayer* to help you along and keep you on track. Watch for directives (rubrics) in small print (in some editions, in red).

For Morning Prayer for the tenth Sunday, you will be using prayer texts from two different places in the book: the Propers (p. 501), and Week II of the Psalter (p. 668). Make use of the colored ribbons provided, or other bookmarks, to help you keep your place in both sections.

Opening

There are two options for opening Morning Prayer:

Option 1

You may begin Morning Prayer with the Invitatory (p. 533). If you choose to do so, the opening is as follows:

Lord, open my lips.
And my mouth will proclaim your praise.
(No "Glory to the Father" follows this opening.)

Then an antiphon is said. For the tenth Sunday of Ordinary time, the antiphon is taken from Week II: "Come, worship the Lord, for we are his people, the flock he shepherds, alleluia" (p. 668). This would be prayed responsorially with the invitatory psalm, in this case, Psalm 95 (pp. 534–535).

Option 2

If the invitatory psalm is not used, the opening is as follows:

God, come to my assistance.
Lord, make haste to help me.
Glory to the Father... (p. 535). The doxology (Glory to the Father) closes with an "alleluia," except during Lent.

Hymn

Some editions of Christian Prayer include a suggested hymn for each day. Other editions provide a collection from which to choose. Other hymns not included in Christian Prayer may be substituted, but they should be appropriate to the time of day and/or the feast or season. In private recitation, you may wish to omit the hymn.

Psalmody

The section referred to as psalmody consists of two psalms and a canticle. For Morning Prayer, the sequence is: psalm, Old Testament canticle, and psalm.

Psalm I

For the tenth Sunday in Ordinary Time, antiphon 1, "Blessed is he who comes...(p. 669), precedes Psalm 118, which concludes with "Glory to the Father..." After a brief pause, the optional psalm-prayer may be recited. The antiphon may be repeated after the psalm-prayer.[6]

Old Testament Canticle

Antiphon 2 for the Old Testament canticle, "Let us sing a hymn..." precedes the Canticle from David, which concludes with "Glory to the Father...." There is no psalm-prayer after canticles, but the antiphon may be repeated. A brief pause before continuing is recommended.

Psalm II

Antiphon 3, "Praise the Lord..." is prayed before Psalm 150, which concludes as usual with the "Glory to the Father...." Again, the psalm may be followed with the optional psalm-prayer, and antiphon 3 may be repeated.

Reading

A selection from Sacred Scripture follows the psalmody. During Ordinary Time, the reading is taken from the day: for the tenth Sunday in Ordinary Time, the reading for Week II is from Ezekiel.

Responsory

An optional response is provided for each reading. In place of the responsory, a period of silence may also be observed. The dialogic structure of the responsory suggests that it is meant for public prayer. However, it can also be prayed privately, with perhaps some adaptation. The response would be prayed in the following manner:

Reader: We give thanks to you, O God,
as we call upon your name.

All: We give thanks to you, O God,
as we call upon your name.

Reader: We cry aloud how marvelous you are.

All: As we call upon your name.
Reader: Glory to the Father and to the Son and to the Holy Spirit.
All: We give thanks to you, O God, as we call upon your name.

This is the usual format. Notice that in the first exchange both *reader* and *all* pray the same text. In the second, the text is divided between the two groups. In the third, only the first half of the "Glory to the Father…," is prayed, and all conclude the responsory by repeating the original line a final time. If you pray the Liturgy of the Hours privately, the repetitions may be omitted.

Gospel Canticle

Turn to the Proper (p. 501) for the antiphon for the tenth Sunday. (You will note that each Sunday has three proper antiphons, one for each of the three primary hours of Sunday.[7]) Turn back to the Psalter for the canticle. The antiphon may be repeated after the "Glory to the Father…," which concludes the canticle.

INTERCESSIONS

The intercessory prayers are designed for communal recitation, but serve equally well for private recitation. There are two ways of praying them:

Option 1

If a presider is leading the prayer, this person begins by reading the invitation: "Let us give thanks...." The refrain in bold print (or in italics in other editions) is recited by all after the invitation.

The presider then prays: "Lord Jesus, you are the rising Sun, the firstfruits of the future resurrection, grant that we may not sit in the shadow of death but walk in the light of life."

All respond with the invocation in bold: "Christ, King of Glory, be our light and our joy," and this manner is repeated throughout the intercessions.

Option 2

The alternate manner for praying the intercessions is to have the presider pray only the first half of each intercession with the congregation coming in at the dash, as follows:

Presider: "Lord Jesus, you are the rising Sun, the firstfruits of the future resurrection,

All: "grant that we may not sit in the shadow of death but walk in the light of life."

With this manner, the refrain is recited only once, after the presider reads the invitation. Spontaneous intercessions may always be added.

Lord's Prayer

The Lord's Prayer concludes the intercessions.

Concluding Prayer

The concluding prayer is taken from the Proper for the tenth Sunday. Some editions of Christian Prayer provide an alternate concluding prayer for Sundays and solemnities.[8]

Dismissal

There are two formulas for the dismissal. The one used depends upon whether or not the presider is ordained. For private recitation, the form begins: "May the Lord bless us…," and can be found in the Ordinary (p. 541).

Night Prayer

The simplest of the Hours, Night Prayer is organized in a one-week cycle (pp. 1008–1045), and is most appropriately prayed just before retiring. After the usual introductory versicle, "God, come to my assistance…" a brief examen of conscience may be made.[9] A hymn may follow the examen, particularly in communal celebrations. Everything follows in order, as provided in *Christian Prayer*. After the closing prayer, one of the antiphons in honor of the Blessed Virgin is prayed or sung. Some editions of *Christian Prayer* include all the options at the end of the Night Prayer section. Pauline Books & Media's edition reprints all of the options for each day. While there is some latitude for choice, the second antiphon, "Loving mother of the Redeemer," is most appropriate for the Advent/Christmas/Epiphany season and "Queen of Heaven" for the Easter season.

Determining the "Observance" of the Day

When you are comfortable with following the general format of Morning, Evening, and Night Prayer, you are ready for the next step: special observances.

In order to pray Morning and Evening Prayer for a special observance you must first determine the Church observance and its "rank." So, while the general structure is the same, there are also specific components determined by the ranking and, very often, several options.

Some publishers of *Christian Prayer* provide an *ordo*[10] with specific page references to their edition. This makes finding the prayer much easier. An ordo tells you whether a particular date is a Sunday, a weekday, a solemnity, a feast day, or some other observance. Nevertheless, it is possible to determine this on one's own.

Ranking or Order of Precedence

Consult the chronological listing of daily celebrations of feasts of Our Lord and the saints for the particular rank of that celebration. Each "rank" follows a particular pattern of prayer elements, and it is best to check the ranking before choosing the various components of the prayer.[11] The rank or order of precedence is as follows:

Solemnity: The highest rank for any day and takes precedence over all other celebrations. Some examples of solemnities include the days of the Sacred Triduum, Christmas, St. Joseph, Husband of Mary, and the Birth of John the Baptist.

Feast: The second highest rank in the Church calendar,[12] these feast days are celebrated with somewhat less festivity than solemnities. Some examples of feasts include the celebrations of most of the apostles, the Transfiguration, and the Birth of Mary.

Memorial: Third in the order of celebrations are memorials, which are obligatory. The calendar requires that these days be observed, as long as there is no conflict with a higher-ranking feast, but the celebration of all Sundays, solemnities, and feasts take precedence over memorials.[13] Many of the observances of the saints are memorials, such as St. Benedict, St. Clare, and the Guardian Angels.

Optional Memorials: If a date on the calendar indicates the remembrance of a saint, but there is no ranking, the observance is optional. When an optional memorial is not observed, the weekday is prayed. During the season of Lent, memorials and optional memorials become commemorations, which are also optional.

Sundays: Sundays are not included in the Roman calendar since they are movable observances. The celebration of Sunday takes precedence over all memorials, most feast days, and some solemnities. Consult a liturgical calendar or ordo for designations for each Sunday.[14]

Weekdays: If there is no designated observance, the current weekday in the four-week Psalter is prayed.

Proper, Common, Weekday

The various elements of liturgical prayer are organized by the terms: proper, common, and weekday. Knowing these will help you to locate the various prayer elements for any given day.

Proper refers to prayers specifically assigned for an occasion. They are printed under the heading of a feast or date. For example, the feast of St. James on July 25 includes several elements of Morning Prayer specific to that feast (pp. 1176–1177). In the same way, the single prayer for the memorial of St. Elizabeth of Hungary, on November 17 (p. 1279) is the Proper closing prayer.

Memorials usually have fewer Proper parts than solemnities or feasts. In a few instances, where devotion to a particular saint is a very ancient tradition, e.g. St. Mary Magdalene, more Propers may be assigned. On the other hand, the solemnities of Christmas and Easter have extensive Propers. All Sundays of the Church year have Proper parts, designated either by the name of a feast, or a number within a season (e.g.,

Second Sunday in Lent, or fifteenth Sunday in Ordinary Time).

Common refers to those prayers that have been composed for a certain category of observances rather than for a single day. For example, the feasts of the apostles share common prayers designated as the Common of Apostles; martyrs the Common of Martyrs; doctors of the Church the Common of Doctors of the Church, etc. Therefore, for the feasts of the Apostle, St. Bartholomew (August 24), and St. Matthew (September 21), the Common of Apostles (pp. 1345–1347) would be used for Morning and Evening Prayer.

Since the Proper *always* takes precedence over the common, it is helpful to first locate all the Proper parts. If no Proper parts are provided, then use the designated common. For example, the feast of St. Bartholomew (p. 1208) provides a Proper closing prayer only. Thus, you would take all other parts from the Common of Apostles.

If you are beginning to feel a little lost, keep a close eye on your *Christian Prayer.* The directions provided in small print will help you to determine which parts to choose. For example, for the feast of St. Bartholomew on August 24, the small print on page 1208 directs you to the Common of Apostles and tells you the page number.

Weekday refers to days on which there is no assigned solemnity, feast, or memorial. The prayer of the day for the current week is prayed.

Finding Morning Prayer and Evening Prayer for Each Day

Now that you have learned the basic structure of Morning and Evening Prayer and the difference between Proper and Common, the next step is to look at the formulas that determine the options for each of the five ranks—solemnities, feasts, memorials, Sundays, and weekdays.[12]

Sundays

Sundays begin at sundown of the evening before the actual date in keeping with the ancient tradition rooted in Jewish practice. Thus,

Evening Prayer on Saturday is called Evening Prayer I of Sunday, and Evening Prayer for Sundays is labeled Evening Prayer II.

You must first determine which week in the four-week cycle is assigned for a particular Sunday. You may wish to consult an ordo or the pamphlet, "Frequently Used Texts and Dates for the Four Week Psalter" published by Pauline Books & Media. You can also determine this if you know that a given Sunday falls within Advent, Lent, Easter, or Ordinary Time, because these seasons always begin with Week I. It follows that the Third Sunday of Lent would use the third week of the cycle and the Fifth Sunday of Easter the first week. In the same way, the second Sunday in Ordinary time follows the second-week cycle and the seventh Sunday in Ordinary time, the third-week cycle, etc. Most editions of *Christian Prayer* also indicate which week of the Psalter to use under the Propers for a given Sunday.

The Proper of Seasons for Sundays refers to the parts of Morning and Evening Prayer that are assigned for that particular Sunday. The Sundays of Ordinary time are assigned two Proper parts for Morning and Evening Prayer: the antiphon for the Gospel Canticle and the closing prayer. Other seasons of the year are assigned additional Proper parts. During the Easter season, for instance, there are Proper antiphons for not only the psalms, but the readings and intercessions as well.

Solemnities

Like Sundays, all solemnities have an Evening Prayer I and an Evening Prayer II. Both Evening Prayers are taken from the Proper or the Common. Thus, Evening Prayer I for the solemnity of St. Joseph is celebrated on the evening of March 18. On the evening of March 19, Evening Prayer II for the solemnity is celebrated.

Morning Prayer for solemnities is taken from the Proper, where provided, or the Common. The Proper for the day will indicate which Common to use. Please take note that the psalms for Morning Prayer on solemnities are always from Sunday, Week I.

Putting this into Practice

At this point, it may be helpful to outline how these guidelines would work in a specific case. We will use the solemnity of All Saints on November 1 as an example.

1. By turning to the General Roman Calendar, you will see that November 1 is the solemnity of All Saints, and that the calendar directs you to page 1262 in *Christian Prayer*.

2. The Propers for the solemnity of All Saints on page 1262 begin with Evening Prayer I for the evening of October 31 (All Hallow's Eve). Since all parts of Evening Prayer I are Proper, the entirety of the text is located here; no other pages need to be consulted.[13] The same holds true for Evening Prayer II; the entire prayer is found under the Proper for November 1 (pp. 1269–1271).

3. Morning Prayer for the solemnity of All Saints, however, is not to be found in one place—in fact, this is true of Morning Prayer for all solemnities. Turn to page 1266 to locate Morning Prayer for November 1. After Antiphon 1, you are directed to turn to page 556 for the psalms of Sunday Morning, Week I—you will be praying the proper antiphons with these psalms. This will involve flipping back and forth between the Proper and Psalter. After the psalmody and accompanying psalm-prayers, turn to the Proper for the reading, responsory, antiphon for the Canticle of Zechariah, intercessions, and closing prayer.

In summary, Solemnities for Evening Prayer I and II will usually have Propers for the entire hour whereas Morning Prayer will involve a combination of Morning Prayer from Sunday, Week I and the Propers for the celebration of that day.

Feast Days

Universal feasts of the Lord that occur on a Sunday begin with Evening Prayer I. The feast of the Transfiguration of Our Lord (August 6) is such a feast. No need to memorize this information, however, since it is mentioned in the Propers for the day. Just be aware that this may occur so that you will be able to begin the celebration the night before.

Locate the Propers for both Morning Prayer and Evening Prayer (if there is no Evening Prayer I and II). Any parts not included are taken from the Commons as directed in the Propers. As with solemnities, Morning Prayer uses the psalms of Sunday, Week I and follows the same format.

Memorials

Memorials have the most options and variation in the way Propers are assigned. Choose the options that require the least amount of paging back and forth, especially when you are just learning.

As a general rule Morning and Evening Prayer use the psalms and their antiphons from the current weekday—one of the key aspects in which memorials differ from solemnities and feasts.

If there are Propers assigned to a memorial, these always take precedence over either a Common or weekday. There is never an option to omit Propers. However, aside from the psalms, which are always from the weekday, the remaining parts of the prayer can be taken from either the Common or the weekday. The simpler choice is the weekday. Many memorials only have a proper closing prayer.

If you choose to pray with the Common, then turn to it only for the reading and response, antiphons for the Gospel Canticle, and intercessions. If you pray the invitatory psalm at the beginning of Morning Prayer, then you may use the antiphon for the invitatory from the Common.

There are about seven exceptions in the current universal calendar, however. These occur when the memorial is assigned Proper antiphons for the psalms. In this case—and in this case only—Sunday Week I psalms are used with proper antiphons instead of the weekday psalms. The psalms assigned for the Commons are prayed for Evening Prayer instead of the weekday psalms. The appearance of Proper antiphons for the psalms is the cue that the Sunday Week I psalms will be prayed rather than the weekday.

Optional Memorials

There is no requirement to observe optional memorials, but you might choose to do so out of a personal devotion to a saint or other reason. The same guidelines for memorials are operative for optional memorials. In general, especially at the beginning, it might be better to omit the optional memorials and focus on the weekday prayer. In addition to simplifying your preparation (less time spent locating options), this will also allow you to discover more clearly the wonderful pattern of daily praise that the cycle of daily psalms, prayers, and readings was designed to be.

In summary, you should first locate the various parts of the hour you are about to pray. The rank will determine whether the psalms are from the weekday or Sunday. All Propers must be included in the prayer. Whenever you have the option, choosing the weekday will enable you to pray with fewer distractions and will attune you to the rhythm of the daily and weekly cycles of the prayer.

Some Final Thoughts

Those who have had the blessing of being introduced to the Liturgy of the Hours, and have grown to love it, are encouraged to share it with others. A good way to begin is to invite a small group to pray a simplified version of the Hours—perhaps beginning with one or two psalms and repeating them on several successive occasions until the group is familiar with the format. Repetition and the reverent and thoughtful celebration of symbols and gestures will enable participants to enter into the rhythm of the prayer with body, mind, and spirit. Keep in mind that the central symbol of the Liturgy of the Hours is *time* and its central theme is *light*. Attentiveness to how these two realities define us as human beings, and how they are reflected in the Scripture and prayers of this liturgy, can enhance the spiritual benefits and enjoyment of the Hours. Consult the *General Instruction on the Liturgy of the Hours* and the various commentaries for further information and suggestions for individual and communal celebration.

Suggestions for Further Reading

Bradshaw, Paul F. "'Cathedral and Monastic' Prayer." *Two Ways of Praying*. Nashville: Abingdon Press, 1995. (scholarly, but accessible)

Brook, John. *The School of Prayer: An Introduction to the Divine Office for All Christians*. Collegeville: The Liturgical Press, 1991.

Brueggemann, Walter. *Praying the Psalms*. Winona, Minnesota: St. Mary's Press, Christian Brothers Publications, 1982. (older work, but significant Scripture scholar; accessible reading)

Campbell, Stanislaus. "Hours, Liturgy of the." In *The New Dictionary of Sacramental Worship*, ed. Peter E. Fink, 562–576. Collegeville: The Liturgical Press, 1990. (scholarly)

Crichton, J.D. *Christian Celebration: The Prayer of the Church*. London: Geoffrey Chapman, 1976. (scholarly, but accessible; key work)

Guiver, George. *Company of Voices: Daily Prayer and the People of God*. New York: Pueblo Publishing Company, 1988. (broader reflection on daily prayer)

Martimort, Aimé Georges. "The Liturgy of the Hours." *The Church at Prayer*. New edition. Vol. IV: *The Liturgy and Time*, ed. Aimé Georges Martimort, Irénée Henri Dalmais, and Pierre Journel, 151–275. Translated by Matthew J. O'Connell. Collegeville: The Liturgical Press, 1986. (scholarly)

Martin, Francis. *The Songs of God's People: The Psalms as Prayer and Poetry*. Denville, New Jersey: Dimension Books, 1978. (popular)

Miller, Charles E. *Together in Prayer: Learning to Love the Liturgy of the Hours*. New York: Alba House, 1994. (popular)

Roquet, A.M. *The Liturgy of the Hours: The General Instruction on the Liturgy of the Hours with Commentary*. Translated by Peter Coughlan and Peter Purdue. Collegeville: The Liturgical Press, 1971. (early work, but key document with an excellent commentary)

Scotto, Dominic F. *The Liturgy of the Hours*. Petersham, Massachusetts: St. Bede's Publications, 1987. (popular)

Taft, Robert. *The Liturgy of the Hours in East and West*. Collegeville: The Liturgical Press, 1986. (scholarly)

Zimmerman, Joyce Ann. *Morning and Evening: A Parish Celebration*. Chicago: Liturgy Training Publications, 1996. (good pastoral resource)

Notes

1. This development resulted in the practice of referring to this prayer as the *Divine Office* or the *Breviary*.

2. Strange as it may seem, this was not necessarily always the case before Vatican II.

3. St. Paul's edition also includes Daytime Prayer in the four-week psalter. Other editions place it in a separate section.

4. St. Paul's edition begins with Sunday and concludes with Saturday. Other editions begin with Saturday and conclude with Friday.

5. It might be helpful for those who are beginners to omit the invitatory psalm, since it is optional, until they have mastered the other parts of the Liturgy of the Hours.

6. In every case, the antiphon may be repeated at the conclusion of a psalm or canticle.

7. It is interesting to note that the antiphon for Evening Prayer I is taken from the Sunday Gospel for cycle A, for Morning Prayer from Cycle B and for Evening Prayer II from Cycle C.

8. Both choices are also the opening prayers of the Eucharist for that day.

9. The rubrics suggest using a penitential rite formula of the Mass for communal celebrations. St. Paul's edition offers some traditional penitential prayer options on pp. 1042–1045.

10. The word *ordo* means "order of worship." It is the set of directions that assists the worshiper in locating the specific elements assigned for each day. When there are options, these are also indicated. If you use an ordo, be sure to use the one published for the current year. Specific guidelines found in the *General Instruction for the Liturgy of the Hours* are also helpful in interpreting the options listed in the *Ordo*. An Ordo will also indicate which week of the four-week cycle to pray, thereby eliminating the need to keep track of the cycle or do the math. General liturgical ordos that publish information about celebrating the eucharist also include information about the Hours. However, it is possible to determine the observance of a given day on one's own with the guidelines that follow.

11. Again, an ordo provides this information.

12. The word "feast" can be used two ways. Either it designates a specific ranking of a celebration or it refers in a generic sense to a celebration of any rank.

13. Under normal circumstances, the calendar has been so arranged that such conflicts are avoided and are therefore not the concern of the individual praying the Hours.

14. Pauline Books & Media publishes a small pamphlet called "Frequently Used Texts and Dates for the Four Week Psalter." This useful aid includes the dates for the four-week psalter and the specific dates in a given year for Sundays, solemnities, and feasts.

The Daughters of St. Paul operate book and media centers at the following addresses. Visit, call or write the one nearest you today, or find us on the World Wide Web, www.pauline.org

CALIFORNIA
3908 Sepulveda Blvd, Culver City, CA 90230 310-397-8676
5945 Balboa Avenue, San Diego, CA 92111 858-565-9181
46 Geary Street, San Francisco, CA 94108 415-781-5180

FLORIDA
145 S.W. 107th Avenue, Miami, FL 33174 305-559-6715

HAWAII
1143 Bishop Street, Honolulu, HI 96813 808-521-2731
Neighbor Islands call: 800-259-8463

ILLINOIS
172 North Michigan Avenue, Chicago, IL 60601 312-346-4228

LOUISIANA
4403 Veterans Memorial Blvd, Metairie, LA 70006 504-887-7631

MASSACHUSETTS
885 Providence Hwy, Dedham, MA 02026 781-326-5385

MISSOURI
9804 Watson Road, St. Louis, MO 63126 314-965-3512

NEW JERSEY
561 U.S. Route 1, Wick Plaza, Edison, NJ 08817 732-572-1200

NEW YORK
150 East 52nd Street, New York, NY 10022 212-754-1110
78 Fort Place, Staten Island, NY 10301 718-447-5071

PENNSYLVANIA
9171-A Roosevelt Blvd, Philadelphia, PA 19114 215-676-9494

SOUTH CAROLINA
243 King Street, Charleston, SC 29401 843-577-0175

TENNESSEE
4811 Poplar Avenue, Memphis, TN 38117 901-761-2987

TEXAS
114 Main Plaza, San Antonio, TX 78205 210-224-8101

VIRGINIA
1025 King Street, Alexandria, VA 22314 703-549-3806

CANADA
3022 Dufferin Street, Toronto, Ontario Canada M6B 3T5 416-781-9131
1155 Yonge Street, Toronto, Ontario, Canada M4T 1W2 416-934-3440

¡También somos su fuente para libros, videos y música en español!